EMMANUEL JOSEPH

The Fashion Industry: A Global Powerhouse with Environmental Consequences

Contents

1

Chapter 1: Introduction

Section 1.1: The Global Fashion Phenomenon

The fashion industry, once a reflection of cultural shifts and societal norms, has transformed into a global powerhouse of economic might and cultural influence. Clothing is no longer a mere necessity but a statement of identity, style, and social status. The allure of new trends, accessible pricing, and constantly evolving collections has turned fashion into a pervasive force, touching every corner of the globe. In the last few decades, the industry has experienced unprecedented growth, giving birth to the era of fast fashion.

Section 1.2: The Rise of Fast Fashion

Fast fashion is a term coined to describe the accelerated production and distribution of inexpensive clothing, inspired by the latest runway styles. Brands and retailers catering to fast fashion can bring new collections to market within weeks, providing consumers with an ever-changing array of options. While this has made fashion more accessible and affordable, it has also introduced a host of environmental challenges.

Section 1.3: The Environmental Consequences

As the fashion industry has expanded, so too have its environmental consequences. The production of textiles, manufacturing processes, transportation, and consumer behavior collectively contribute to a significant ecological footprint. The fast fashion model relies on the rapid turnover of clothing items, which encourages the disposal of old garments and the acquisition of new ones. This cycle results in a massive waste problem and a host of environmental concerns.

Section 1.4: Purpose and Scope of This Study

This study seeks to explore and understand the environmental impact of the fashion industry, particularly focusing on the repercussions of fast fashion. It will delve into the environmental challenges associated with different stages of clothing production and consumption, from textile manufacturing to disposal. Additionally, it aims to highlight the need for sustainable clothing production as a countermeasure to the industry's environmental degradation.

Section 1.5: Chapter Overview

To achieve these objectives, this chapter sets the stage for the entire study. The subsequent chapters will provide in-depth analysis and solutions, but this introductory chapter serves as a foundation. In the chapters to follow, we will explore the historical context of fashion, the environmental impact of textile production, the life cycle of garments, and consumption patterns that drive the fashion industry. We will also delve into the role of marketing and advertising, dissect the fashion supply chain, discuss the industry's contribution to climate change, and assess the effects of water usage and pollution. The study will also shed light on waste and recycling in the fashion sector, sustainable practices that offer alternatives, and the roadmap to a more sustainable future.

Through these explorations, it becomes evident that the fashion industry is at a crossroads, where environmental responsibility must be integrated into the very fabric of its existence. This is not only a matter of ecological preservation but also one of social and economic significance. The transformation of the fashion industry toward sustainability is not only desirable but essential for the well-being of our planet and future generations. This study will navigate the multifaceted challenges and opportunities on this path toward a more sustainable fashion industry.

2

Chapter 2: Historical Context

Section 2.1: A Journey Through Time

Fashion, as we know it today, has undergone a remarkable evolution over the centuries. To comprehend the current environmental challenges posed by the industry, it is essential to trace its historical roots. Clothing has been a fundamental aspect of human existence, dating back to our ancestors who draped themselves in animal hides and plant fibers for protection and warmth.

Section 2.2: The Roots of Slow Fashion

In the past, clothing was predominantly crafted by hand, with painstaking attention to detail, quality, and durability. This era can be referred to as "slow fashion." Garments were made to last, often handed down through generations. The materials used were limited, sourced locally, and had a minimal environmental footprint. In this era, clothing was more about necessity than disposable fashion.

Section 2.3: Industrial Revolution and the Birth of Fast Fashion

The turning point in the fashion industry's history came with the Industrial

Revolution. The mechanization of textile production and the advent of factory-based manufacturing significantly increased the speed and scale of clothing production. Mass-produced textiles and garments became more affordable and accessible to the masses, ushering in the era of fast fashion.

Section 2.4: Post-World War II and Consumerism

After World War II, consumerism in Western societies began to rise significantly. Economic prosperity and cultural shifts led to the idea of regularly updating one's wardrobe with the latest styles. The fashion industry capitalized on this growing demand by offering a wide array of clothing options at affordable prices.

Section 2.5: Globalization and the Digital Age

The late 20th and early 21st centuries witnessed further transformation in the fashion industry. Globalization made it possible to source materials and labor from around the world, leading to a complex and interconnected fashion supply chain. The digital age revolutionized shopping, with online retailers and social media influencing fashion trends and consumer behavior.

Section 2.6: The Dark Side of Fashion's Evolution

As fashion evolved, so did its environmental impact. The transition from slow fashion to fast fashion has brought about resource-intensive manufacturing processes, enormous textile waste, and the proliferation of synthetic fibers. The breakneck pace of production and consumption has pushed the industry to the forefront of global environmental issues.

Section 2.7: Lessons from History

Understanding the historical context of fashion allows us to draw critical lessons. It highlights the fact that fashion has not always been synonymous with disposability and environmental degradation. Slow fashion traditions emphasized craftsmanship, durability, and local sourcing - principles that the modern fashion industry can draw from in its quest for sustainability.

By examining this historical evolution, we can better appreciate how we arrived at the environmental challenges the fashion industry faces today. This understanding will inform our exploration of solutions and alternatives in subsequent chapters, guiding the industry toward a more sustainable future.

3

Chapter 3: Environmental Impact of Textile Production

Section 3.1: The Beginning of the Fashion Supply Chain

Textile production forms the critical foundation of the fashion supply chain. In this chapter, we delve into the first stage of clothing manufacturing, examining the environmental consequences that emerge during the creation of the very fabrics that make up our garments.

Section 3.2: The Ecological Footprint of Textile Fibers

Different textile fibers have distinct environmental impacts. This section dissects various types of fibers, such as cotton, polyester, and natural fibers like wool and silk. It examines their cultivation, manufacturing processes, and their contribution to resource consumption and pollution.

Section 3.3: Water Usage and Pollution

The textile industry is notorious for its water-intensive processes. This section explores the staggering amounts of water used in dyeing and finishing textiles, and the pollutants released into water bodies. It also highlights the global water scarcity issues exacerbated by textile production.

Section 3.4: Chemicals and Hazardous Substances

Textile manufacturing relies on a wide array of chemicals, from dyes and bleaches to finishing agents. We discuss the detrimental effects of these chemicals on the environment, including their persistence in the ecosystem and the health hazards they pose to workers.

Section 3.5: Energy Consumption in Textile Production

Textile mills and factories are energy-intensive operations. We delve into the vast amounts of energy consumed in the spinning, weaving, and finishing processes, shedding light on the carbon footprint of textile production.

Section 3.6: Waste and Byproducts

Textile production generates significant waste, including cuttings, off-cuts, and defective products. This section explores the challenges of textile waste disposal and highlights how many of these byproducts end up in landfills, contributing to pollution and resource depletion.

Section 3.7: Sustainable Alternatives in Textile Production

Amidst the gloomy environmental picture, there are innovative and sustainable approaches emerging in textile production. We discuss eco-friendly practices like organic cotton farming, water-saving dyeing techniques, and closed-loop systems that aim to minimize the industry's environmental impact.

Section 3.8: Consumer Awareness and Textile Choices

The choices consumers make when purchasing clothing can also influence the textile industry. This section emphasizes the role of consumer awareness and the importance of sustainable material choices in fashion.

Section 3.9: Government Regulations and Industry Initiatives

Government regulations and industry initiatives play a pivotal role in mitigating the environmental impact of textile production. We explore examples of regulations and initiatives that are pushing the industry toward more sustainable practices.

Understanding the environmental impact of textile production is a fundamental step in recognizing the fashion industry's contribution to environmental issues. This chapter lays the groundwork for the subsequent chapters, which will delve into the impact of textile production on the entire fashion supply chain, from design to distribution, and ultimately guide the industry toward sustainable clothing production.

4

Chapter 4: The Life Cycle of a Garment

Section 4.1: From Cradle to Grave

In this chapter, we explore the entire life cycle of a garment, from its creation to its eventual disposal. Understanding the different stages in a garment's existence is crucial for identifying the environmental impact at each step.

Section 4.2: Design and Development

The journey of a garment begins with its design. We examine how the choices made during this phase, including materials, production processes, and durability, significantly influence the environmental footprint of the final product.

Section 4.3: Manufacturing and Production

This section discusses the actual creation of the garment, where the fabric is cut, stitched, and assembled. The manufacturing process is a crucial point in the life cycle, impacting energy use, waste generation, and labor conditions.

Section 4.4: Distribution and Transportation

Garments must travel from factories to retail stores and ultimately into the hands of consumers. We look at the energy and emissions associated with transportation and the importance of efficient logistics.

Section 4.5: Consumer Use and Care

Once purchased, the environmental responsibility shifts to the consumer. We discuss how consumer behavior, such as laundering and care practices, can extend the lifespan of a garment or contribute to its early disposal.

Section 4.6: Repair, Upcycling, and Alterations

Extending the life of a garment is key to sustainability. This section explores repair, upcycling, and alteration as eco-friendly alternatives to discarding clothing.

Section 4.7: Secondhand and Vintage Markets

Secondhand and vintage markets are growing, presenting sustainable options for consumers. We discuss the significance of these markets in reducing the environmental impact of fashion.

Section 4.8: End of Life and Disposal

When garments reach the end of their useful life, they are often discarded. We analyze the impact of garment disposal, including the environmental consequences of textile waste in landfills.

Section 4.9: Circular Fashion and Sustainable Cycles

Circular fashion concepts are gaining traction. This section explores strategies like recycling, repurposing, and closed-loop systems that aim to minimize waste and create sustainable cycles in the fashion industry.

Section 4.10: The Role of Technology and Innovation

Innovations in materials and technologies play a vital role in extending the lifespan of clothing and reducing the environmental impact. We highlight advancements in sustainable textiles and manufacturing methods.

Section 4.11: Consumer Education and Responsibility

A sustainable fashion industry requires an informed and responsible consumer base. We discuss the importance of consumer education and awareness in promoting responsible clothing use and disposal.

Section 4.12: Industry Responsibility and Extended Producer Responsibility

The fashion industry also bears a significant responsibility for the garments it creates. We explore concepts like extended producer responsibility, which places the onus on manufacturers to manage products through their entire life cycle.

By comprehensively examining the life cycle of a garment, we gain insight into the critical stages where sustainability efforts can be most effective. This understanding guides the industry toward making more responsible choices at every point in a garment's existence and helps consumers make informed decisions that reduce the environmental impact of their clothing choices.

5

Chapter 5: Consumption Patterns and Overconsumption

Section 5.1: The Thrill of Newness

Consumer behavior has a profound impact on the fashion industry's environmental footprint. This chapter delves into the psychology of fashion consumption and the desire for new and trendy clothing.

Section 5.2: The Disposable Fashion Culture

The fashion industry's fast-paced model has cultivated a culture of disposability. This section explores the idea of wearing a garment a few times and then discarding it, contributing to the vast amount of textile waste.

Section 5.3: Social Media and Consumer Influences

Social media platforms and influencers play a significant role in shaping consumer trends and influencing purchasing decisions. We discuss how these platforms perpetuate a need for constant newness and fast fashion.

Section 5.4: Fast Fashion Business Models

Fast fashion brands use marketing strategies that encourage frequent purchases. This section analyzes the business models of these brands and their impact on consumer behavior.

Section 5.5: The Psychology of Consumerism

Consumerism extends beyond the desire for new clothes. We delve into the psychological and emotional aspects of consumer behavior, exploring the role of identity, self-esteem, and social validation.

Section 5.6: Psychological Triggers and Advertising

Fashion advertisements often employ psychological triggers to entice consumers. This section uncovers how advertising techniques exploit emotions and desires, leading to impulsive buying.

Section 5.7: Ethical and Sustainable Consumer Choices

Consumers are increasingly aware of the environmental and ethical issues in the fashion industry. We highlight the emergence of ethical and sustainable fashion choices and their significance in countering overconsumption.

Section 5.8: Minimalism and Slow Fashion Movements

Minimalism and slow fashion movements promote a shift away from the culture of overconsumption. We explore these alternative consumer philosophies and their impact on the industry.

Section 5.9: Repair, Reuse, and Longevity

The concept of making clothing last is gaining traction. We discuss the importance of repairing and extending the lifespan of garments, fostering a culture of longevity over disposability.

Section 5.10: The Role of Education and Awareness

Consumer education is essential in promoting responsible fashion choices. We examine the role of education and awareness campaigns in cultivating more mindful and sustainable consumer behavior.

Section 5.11: Government Policies and Regulations

Governments can influence consumption patterns through policies and regulations. We explore examples of policy measures aimed at curbing overconsumption and encouraging sustainability.

Section 5.12: The Path to Responsible Consumption

In the face of overconsumption and its environmental consequences, this section discusses the path to responsible consumption, advocating for a shift in mindset from quantity to quality, from disposability to sustainability.

Understanding the psychological and cultural factors that drive consumer behavior in the fashion industry is crucial for implementing change. This chapter not only analyzes the challenges posed by overconsumption but also offers insights into the potential for a more sustainable fashion culture where consumers make thoughtful choices that benefit both the environment and society.

6

Chapter 6: The Role of Marketing and Advertising

Section 6.1: The Power of Visual Messaging

Marketing and advertising have played a pivotal role in shaping the fashion industry and influencing consumer choices. This chapter delves into the ways in which visual messaging impacts fashion consumption.

Section 6.2: Branding and Aspirational Imagery

Fashion brands often use aspirational imagery to create a desire for their products. We examine how branding influences consumer perceptions and encourages the pursuit of a particular lifestyle.

Section 6.3: Social Media and Digital Marketing

The advent of social media has transformed the fashion advertising landscape. We explore how platforms like Instagram, Pinterest, and TikTok have become powerful tools for fashion marketing, shaping trends and consumer behavior.

Section 6.4: Fast Fashion Advertising Strategies

Fast fashion brands employ specific advertising strategies to drive rapid sales and frequent turnover of inventory. We analyze techniques such as flash sales, limited-time offers, and constant product turnover.

Section 6.5: Greenwashing and Ethical Marketing

The fashion industry has seen an increase in greenwashing – the practice of presenting a false or exaggerated image of environmental responsibility. This section examines the ethical marketing practices that promote sustainability while distinguishing them from greenwashing.

Section 6.6: Influencers and Their Impact

Influencers have become a powerful force in fashion marketing. We discuss how these individuals shape consumer choices and how brands leverage influencer marketing to reach wider audiences.

Section 6.7: The Push for Transparency

Consumers increasingly demand transparency in marketing and advertising. This section highlights the importance of disclosing manufacturing and sourcing practices and their impact on sustainability.

Section 6.8: Ethical Advertising and Sustainable Fashion Campaigns

Brands and organizations are launching ethical advertising and sustainable fashion campaigns. We showcase examples of campaigns that promote responsible consumption and production.

Section 6.9: Consumer Response and Activism

The role of consumers in shaping fashion advertising is explored. We discuss instances of consumer activism and how social media has given individuals a platform to call out unethical marketing practices.

Section 6.10: Industry Shifts Toward Ethical Marketing

The fashion industry is undergoing changes in response to consumer demands for ethical marketing. This section examines how industry players are shifting their marketing strategies to align with sustainability and transparency.

Section 6.11: The Potential for Positive Change

While marketing and advertising have historically been a part of the problem, they can also be a significant part of the solution. We discuss the potential for these tools to educate and inspire consumers to make responsible fashion choices.

This chapter sheds light on the role of marketing and advertising in shaping consumer behavior and fashion industry practices. It emphasizes the need for ethical and sustainable marketing to promote responsible consumption and production.

7

Chapter 7: The Fashion Supply Chain

Section 7.1: The Complex Web of Production

The fashion supply chain is a vast, intricate web that connects raw materials to the end consumer. In this chapter, we explore the various stages and components of this supply chain.

Section 7.2: Raw Materials Sourcing

We begin by examining the starting point of the supply chain: the sourcing of raw materials. This section discusses the significance of sustainable and ethical sourcing practices.

Section 7.3: Textile Manufacturing and Production

Moving down the supply chain, we focus on the manufacturing and production processes that transform raw materials into fabrics and materials for clothing. The environmental impact of these processes is analyzed.

Section 7.4: Globalization and Outsourcing

Globalization has played a pivotal role in shaping the fashion supply chain.

We delve into the consequences of outsourcing production to countries with lower labor and environmental standards.

Section 7.5: Working Conditions and Labor Rights

The fashion supply chain is notorious for poor working conditions and labor rights violations. We examine the challenges faced by workers in the industry and the push for fair labor practices.

Section 7.6: Logistics and Transportation

The movement of products through the supply chain involves transportation and logistics. We discuss the environmental impact of shipping and the importance of efficient transportation.

Section 7.7: Distribution and Retail

The supply chain culminates in the distribution and retail of fashion products. We analyze the implications of the retail environment, including factors like store design and online shopping.

Section 7.8: Inventory Management and Waste

Fashion brands must manage inventory to minimize waste. This section explores inventory practices, including overproduction and disposal of unsold items.

Section 7.9: The Role of Technology in Supply Chain Management

Technology and data analytics are reshaping supply chain management. We highlight how these tools can be harnessed for greater sustainability.

Section 7.10: Sustainable Supply Chain Practices

Many industry players are embracing sustainable supply chain practices. We discuss initiatives, such as ethical sourcing, responsible manufacturing, and efficient logistics, that reduce the environmental impact.

Section 7.11: The Push for Transparency and Traceability

Consumers increasingly demand transparency and traceability in the supply chain. We explore how technology and blockchain are enabling these features.

Section 7.12: The Future of the Fashion Supply Chain

The chapter concludes by looking at the future of the fashion supply chain. We discuss how innovations and changes in practices can lead to a more sustainable and ethical fashion industry.

Understanding the intricacies of the fashion supply chain is pivotal for implementing change in the industry. This chapter delves into the environmental and social consequences of the supply chain while highlighting opportunities for sustainability and ethical practices.

8

Chapter 8: Fashion Industry and Climate Change

Section 8.1: Fashion's Contribution to Greenhouse Gas Emissions

In this chapter, we delve into the fashion industry's significant role in contributing to greenhouse gas emissions. We examine the various aspects of clothing production and consumption that drive climate change.

Section 8.2: Carbon Footprint of Textile Production

Textile production, including the creation of fibers and fabrics, consumes substantial energy and releases greenhouse gases. This section analyzes the carbon footprint of textile manufacturing and the reliance on non-renewable resources.

Section 8.3: Transportation Emissions

The fashion supply chain involves the transportation of raw materials, components, and finished products across the globe. We explore the environmental impact of this extensive transportation network.

Section 8.4: Energy Use in Retail and Storage

Retail spaces and warehouses consume considerable energy. We discuss how energy use in these areas contributes to the industry's carbon footprint.

Section 8.5: The Consumer's Carbon Impact

Consumer behavior, including frequent clothing purchases and laundry practices, plays a significant role in fashion's carbon footprint. We examine how consumer choices affect greenhouse gas emissions.

Section 8.6: Climate Change and Fashion Vulnerabilities

Climate change poses risks to the fashion industry as well. We explore how changing weather patterns, extreme events, and resource scarcity impact the industry's sustainability.

Section 8.7: Sustainable Practices to Mitigate Climate Impact

The fashion industry has the potential to mitigate its climate impact through sustainable practices. This section highlights strategies like eco-friendly materials, energy-efficient production, and responsible consumer choices.

Section 8.8: Innovations in Climate-Responsive Fashion

Innovation is driving climate-responsive fashion. We discuss the emergence of adaptive clothing and textiles that respond to changing environmental conditions.

Section 8.9: Collaborative Efforts and Climate Commitments

Governments, organizations, and fashion brands are making climate commitments. We explore collaborative efforts and initiatives aimed at reducing the industry's carbon footprint.

Section 8.10: The Role of Circular Fashion

Circular fashion practices can significantly reduce the carbon impact of the industry. We discuss how recycling, upcycling, and waste reduction can address climate change concerns.

Section 8.11: Climate-Positive Fashion Futures

The fashion industry has the potential to not only reduce its impact but also become climate-positive. We discuss visions of a fashion future that actively contributes to mitigating climate change.

Understanding the fashion industry's contributions to climate change is crucial in addressing one of the most pressing global issues. This chapter provides an in-depth analysis of the environmental consequences of fashion's carbon footprint and offers insights into the strategies and innovations that can help the industry transition toward climate-friendly practices.

9

Chapter 9: Water Usage and Pollution

Section 9.1: The Thirsty Industry

Water is an essential resource for textile production and the fashion industry. In this chapter, we delve into the extensive water usage and the environmental repercussions of this reliance.

Section 9.2: The Water-Intensive Nature of Textile Dyeing and Finishing

Dyeing and finishing textiles require substantial water quantities. We explore the water-intensive processes in textile manufacturing and the associated pollution.

Section 9.3: The Impact on Local Water Sources

Fashion manufacturing often takes place in regions where water is already scarce. We examine how the industry's water consumption can strain local water sources and exacerbate water scarcity issues.

Section 9.4: Water Pollution and Chemicals

Textile manufacturing releases pollutants and chemicals into water bodies.

This section discusses the environmental hazards of water pollution and its impact on ecosystems and communities.

Section 9.5: The Role of Wastewater Management in Fashion

Wastewater management is a critical aspect of mitigating the industry's water pollution. We highlight the importance of responsible wastewater treatment and recycling.

Section 9.6: Sustainable Dyeing and Finishing Practices

Sustainable alternatives to traditional dyeing and finishing practices are emerging. We discuss innovative techniques that reduce water usage and pollution.

Section 9.7: Water-Saving and Water-Positive Brands

Fashion brands are taking steps to become water-saving or water-positive. We explore examples of companies that have implemented responsible water practices.

Section 9.8: Consumer Choices and Water Conservation

Consumer choices can also influence water conservation in the fashion industry. This section emphasizes the role of consumers in reducing the environmental impact of clothing production.

Section 9.9: Government Regulations and Water Policies

Government regulations and policies can shape water practices in the industry. We analyze examples of water-related regulations and their potential to drive change.

Section 9.10: The Path to Sustainable Water Use in Fashion

Sustainable water practices are essential for the fashion industry's future. We discuss the path toward more responsible water use, including reducing consumption, managing pollution, and ensuring equitable access to water resources.

Understanding the fashion industry's extensive water use and its implications for water resources is pivotal in addressing environmental concerns. This chapter provides a comprehensive overview of the industry's relationship with water and highlights the strategies and practices that can lead to more sustainable water usage in fashion.

10

Chapter 10: Waste and Recycling in Fashion

Section 10.1: The Garbage Problem

Waste is an inherent issue in the fashion industry. In this chapter, we explore the generation of textile waste and its impact on the environment.

Section 10.2: The Extent of Textile Waste

The fashion industry produces an enormous amount of waste, from off-cuts and defective items in production to discarded garments by consumers. We analyze the scale of this waste problem.

Section 10.3: Landfills and Environmental Consequences

Much of textile waste ends up in landfills, contributing to environmental problems. We discuss the ecological consequences of fashion waste in landfills.

Section 10.4: Slow Decomposition of Clothing

Clothing made from synthetic materials can take hundreds of years to decompose. We explore the challenges of these slow-degrading textiles in waste management.

Section 10.5: The Secondhand Clothing Trade

The secondhand clothing market plays a crucial role in waste reduction. We examine the significance of thrift stores and the resale of clothing.

Section 10.6: The Potential of Recycling in Fashion

Recycling is a promising solution to fashion waste. We discuss the potential of recycling materials, including textiles, to reduce the environmental impact of the industry.

Section 10.7: Innovative Recycling Technologies

Innovative recycling technologies are emerging in the fashion sector. We highlight advancements in textile recycling and the creation of new garments from old materials.

Section 10.8: Upcycling and Repurposing

Upcycling and repurposing offer creative solutions to fashion waste. We discuss how old clothing can be transformed into new, stylish items.

Section 10.9: Circular Fashion Practices and Closed-Loop Systems

Circular fashion practices aim to minimize waste. We explore the concept of closed-loop systems, where products are designed for reuse and recycling.

Section 10.10: Consumer Engagement in Recycling and Upcycling

Consumer engagement is crucial in reducing fashion waste. We discuss the importance of consumer participation in recycling and upcycling initiatives.

Section 10.11: The Path to a Waste-Reduced Fashion Industry

To address the waste issue, the fashion industry must adopt waste-reduction strategies. We outline the path to a waste-reduced fashion sector, which includes responsible production, consumer education, and innovative recycling.

This chapter sheds light on the significant problem of waste in the fashion industry and explores various strategies, from recycling to upcycling, that can minimize the environmental consequences of fashion waste.

11

Chapter 11: Sustainable Fashion Practices

Section 11.1: The Rise of Sustainable Fashion

Sustainable fashion practices have gained momentum in response to the environmental challenges posed by the industry. In this chapter, we explore the principles and innovations that characterize the sustainable fashion movement.

Section 11.2: Eco-Friendly Materials and Fabrics

Sustainable fashion often begins with the materials used. We discuss eco-friendly alternatives such as organic cotton, bamboo, and recycled fabrics and their reduced environmental impact.

Section 11.3: Ethical Labor Practices

Ethical labor practices are a cornerstone of sustainable fashion. We explore the importance of fair wages, safe working conditions, and respect for workers' rights.

Section 11.4: Local and Small-Scale Production

Supporting local and small-scale production can reduce the carbon footprint of fashion. We examine the benefits of local sourcing and production.

Section 11.5: Reduced Resource Consumption and Waste

Sustainable fashion minimizes resource use and waste. We discuss practices like zero-waste pattern making and lean production techniques that reduce the industry's environmental impact.

Section 11.6: Repair and Longevity

Extending the lifespan of clothing is a key aspect of sustainability. We explore repair and maintenance practices that allow consumers to keep garments in use for longer.

Section 11.7: Responsible Retail and Distribution

Sustainable fashion extends to retail and distribution. We discuss eco-friendly store designs, responsible packaging, and efficient transportation.

Section 11.8: Transparency and Traceability

Transparency and traceability are essential in sustainable fashion. We highlight the importance of disclosing product information, including sourcing and production details.

Section 11.9: Sustainable Fashion Brands and Initiatives

Many brands are embracing sustainability. We showcase examples of brands and initiatives that prioritize eco-friendly, ethical, and sustainable practices.

Section 11.10: Consumer Education and Ethical Choices

Consumer education is a vital aspect of sustainable fashion. We explore how informed consumers can make ethical choices and support sustainable brands.

Section 11.11: The Business Case for Sustainability

Sustainability is not just an ethical choice but also a sound business strategy. We discuss the business benefits of sustainable fashion, including consumer demand and brand reputation.

Section 11.12: The Road to a More Sustainable Fashion Industry

The chapter concludes by discussing the road to a more sustainable fashion industry. We highlight the collective efforts of brands, consumers, and the industry as a whole in shaping a more environmentally responsible and ethical sector.

Sustainable fashion practices offer a pathway to mitigate the environmental and social challenges posed by the fashion industry. This chapter explores the various components of sustainable fashion, showcasing the potential for a more responsible and eco-friendly fashion future.

12

Chapter 12: The Path to a Sustainable Fashion Future

Section 12.1: The Urgency of Change

This concluding chapter underscores the urgency of addressing the environmental and social issues that plague the fashion industry. It emphasizes the imperative for immediate action and transformative change.

Section 12.2: A Call for Collaboration

Solving the complex challenges of the fashion industry requires collaboration among stakeholders. We discuss the need for collective action from governments, businesses, consumers, and advocacy groups.

Section 12.3: The Role of Government and Policy

Government policies and regulations can be instrumental in reshaping the fashion industry. We explore the potential impact of environmental and labor regulations on fashion practices.

Section 12.4: Industry Initiatives and Sustainable Standards

The industry is witnessing the emergence of various initiatives and sustainable standards. We highlight examples of industry-led efforts that promote sustainable practices.

Section 12.5: The Power of Consumer Choices

Consumers hold significant influence over the fashion industry. We discuss the importance of consumer choices in driving demand for sustainable products.

Section 12.6: The Responsibility of Brands and Retailers

Fashion brands and retailers bear a substantial responsibility in steering the industry toward sustainability. We explore the role of brands in adopting ethical and eco-friendly practices.

Section 12.7: Innovation and Technology

Innovation and technology offer the potential for transformative change in fashion. We discuss advancements in materials, production processes, and sustainable solutions.

Section 12.8: Education and Awareness Campaigns

Education and awareness campaigns play a pivotal role in shaping consumer behavior and industry practices. We emphasize the need for ongoing initiatives to inform and engage consumers.

Section 12.9: Creating a Circular Fashion Economy

The transition to a circular fashion economy is a key element of a sustainable future. We discuss how recycling, upcycling, and waste reduction can transform the industry.

Section 12.10: Accountability and Transparency

Accountability and transparency are crucial in ensuring that sustainability goals are met. We highlight the importance of honest reporting and traceability in fashion.

Section 12.11: Sustainable Fashion as a Cultural Shift

Sustainability in fashion is not just about changing practices but also reshaping cultural norms. We discuss how the fashion industry can lead a cultural shift toward responsible consumption and production.

Section 12.12: A Vision for a Sustainable Fashion Future

The chapter concludes by envisioning a sustainable fashion future. We explore what the industry could look like when it embraces environmentally friendly and ethical practices, offering hope for a more responsible and conscientious fashion sector.

The path to a sustainable fashion future is both a challenge and an opportunity. This chapter emphasizes the need for immediate and collective action, addressing the multifaceted challenges of the fashion industry, and highlights the potential for transformation toward a more responsible and sustainable fashion sector.

www.ingramcontent.com/pod-product-compliance
Lightning Source LLC
La Vergne TN
LVHW010837200726
843508LV00012B/2630